Journey Into Literacy

A Workbook For Parents And Teachers Of Young Children

Barbara E. R. Swaby
Illustrated By
Susan Gillings

D1608810

2005
Swaby Books Publisher
1533 Cragin Road
Colorado Springs, CO 80920
719-532-1506

2005
Swaby Books Publisher
1533 Cragin Road
Colorado Springs, CO 80920
719-532-1506

ISBN 1-881897-00-1

Contents

Dedicated to my son, David

Using This Workbook

This book was written specifically for those who work with or raise young children. It is designed to assist adults in understanding and constructing literate environments in the home and at school. At best, the book should be used as a real workbook in that you are encouraged to write in it, take notes in it, keep track of your successes, plan your program and add new information, insights and material as the need arises. It should actually be your own personalized literacy journal for you and your child or children.

Following each chapter is a section titled Personal Record. These pages are designed to provide you with space to add to each booklist, and to keep a record of any comments, thoughts or insights that may be related to the information in each chapter.

Your purchase of this book clearly demonstrates your willingness to create a dynamic and effective literacy environment for children. This book will help you achieve your goal.

1 THE LITERACY CRISIS IN THE UNITED STATES

What is literacy? Is it important? Whose job or whose responsibility is it? How is it achieved? These are all important questions about which all adults need to be concerned. The term literacy as it is used in this workbook refers to the ability to perform successfully on reading and writing tasks. There are four generally accepted levels of literacy: illiteracy, functional literacy, advanced literacy and alliteracy. Illiteracy refers to the state of being unable to read on the most basic level. Individuals who are illiterate are not able to read common signs, labels and notes. They cannot read above the second or early third grade level. According to Jonathan Kozel, renown author of the book *Illiterate America*, approximately 25 million American adults are at this level.(Jonathan Kozel, "Illiteracy Statistics: A Numbers Game," "New York Times," 30 October,1986, p. 27) Functional literacy specifies the level at which individuals are able to read well enough to function in society. They can read their local newspapers, popular magazines such as "People" or "T. V. Guide", and digest magazines such as "Reader's Digest." They find it difficult to read any material of a technical nature. They have attained a reading level of approximately sixth or seventh grade. Again, Kozel estimates that there are about 60 million Americans who are below this level. Advanced literacy refers to the level at which one can read and understand complex texts and highly technical work-related written material. Individuals at this level can read and understand sophisticated national magazines such as "Time" and "Newsweek." There are approximately 72 million Americans who are operating below this level. Alliteracy refers to the state of having the skills of reading, but lacking the desire or motivation to do so. Unfortunately, most of the adult American public would fall in this category. True literacy, then, refers to the ability to read, as well as the willingness and motivation to do so. Is there a literacy problem in the United States? There really is no question about the response. There certainly is! Perhaps the most alarming statistic related to literacy is reported by Nancy Larrick in the Phi Delta Kappan journal, November, 1987. It is estimated that each year, approximately 2.3 million high school students leave school without having achieved the level of functional literacy.

All adults would immediately agree that they desire advanced literacy levels for all children. But how is literacy accomplished? Who holds responsibility for its development? One of the most meaningful explanations of literacy and its development was written by Frank G. Jennings, a former education consultant to *New World Foundation* and editor at large for the "Saturday Review." Jennings' statement titled, "What Is Reading?" places the issue of literacy in clearest perspective. The statement reads:

What Is Reading?

What is reading? Where does it start? How can it be done well? With these questions, you can make a fortune, wreck a school system or get elected to the board of education. Most people who try to think about reading at all, conjure up these little black wriggles on a page and then mutter something about "meaning." If this is all it is, very few of us would ever learn anything. For reading is older than printing, or writing, or even language itself. Reading begins with wonder at the world about us. It starts with an ache that vanished with food or water. It occurs when time is discovered. Reading begins with the management of signs of things. It begins when the mother, holding the child's hand, says that the day is "beautiful," or "cold," or that the wind is "soft." Reading is "signs and portents, "the flight of birds, the changing moon, the changeless sun, and the fixed stars that move through the night. Reading is the practical management of the world around us. It was this for the man at the cave's mouth. It is this at the desk, the bench or the control panel.

The special kind of reading that you are doing now is the culmination of all the other kinds of reading. You are dealing with the signs of the things represented. You are dealing with ideas and concepts that have no material matter or substance and yet are "real". But you cannot do this kind of reading if you have not been skilled in all the other kinds. Unless you know down from up, hot from cold, now from then, you could never learn to understand things that merely represent other things. You would have no language as you now understand it, and you could not live in the open society of human beings. (From *This Is Reading* by Frank G. Jennings, Bureau of Publications, Teachers College, Columbia University, New York, N.Y. 1965, pp3-4). This statement about reading certainly supports the idea that literacy begins in the home and is extended in all societal settings including the school.

Certainly literacy development is related to the amount of time adults spend nurturing and fostering language in children. It has to do with spending time talking and reading to and with children. We as adults must face up to the fact that in our country, most children, prior to entering kindergarten, spend more than 1500 hours watching television, yet they have spent fewer than 60 hours being read to. Nancy Larrick reminds us that children ages 6 to 11 watch a weekly average of 23 hours of television year round. Yet, if children were required to do five hours of homework each week, both parents and children would probably be up in arms.

Literacy has always been a valued goal in most societies. It has been one of the important requisites of the work force. As we move into the technological era, however, the importance of literacy escalates. We are rapidly approaching the year 2000, and the demands of the world of work continue to become more acute. It is easy to see that our children will need to be extremely well prepared in order to meet the requirements of society. Can we be sure that the schools alone can prepare our children for their futures? The achievement of literacy will be a reality only when all adults, parents and teachers, join forces.

The remainder of this book will discuss the environment that encourages literacy and the activities that lead us all on our journey into literacy.

2 ON BECOMING LITERATE: UNDERSTANDING LANGUAGE DEVELOPMENT

The first step in creating a dynamic, literate environment at home or school is understanding the process of language development. If you understand how language happens, it will be easy to see how you can use that information to foster reading development.

We as human beings do four things with language. We listen to it, we speak it, we read it and we write it. The first two behaviors, listening and speaking, are the most basic, and are the skills that set us apart in the animal kingdom. They make us human. We come into this world with all that we need to develop language. It is a natural phenomenon. At first, we listen to the language. Listening forms the base upon which we build speaking. Listening and speaking both form the base for reading. Finally, listening, speaking and reading create the base for writing.

But how does this language develop? How does it happen that we come into the world with clean slates, so to speak, and without any direct instruction whatever, we learn complex rules of language? In addition, how does it happen that within five years, we become very capable language users?

Oral language develops in human beings within three major stages: languaging to children, languaging with children and languaging by children. These three stages will be discussed fully in this chapter.

Language Done To Children

Think back to the time that your children began to learn language. You will remember three clearly identifiable stages. The first stage began at birth and continued through nine to eighteen months. During this time, there was no real speech. The second stage began between nine and eighteen months and ended at about four or five years. During this time, children developed their oral language at a very fast rate. The third stage started at about four or five years and continued throughout the elementary grades.

Let us take a closer look at stage one. This stage is called the languaging to stage. It gets its name from the behaviors of mature language users in the environments of infants. During this stage, children's ears do the work: listening is the key.

Let us analyze the characteristics of this first stage. Think of the ways in which you interacted with your children from birth to the time they spoke their first real words. This stage has some clear and important characteristics:

- Children are immersed in language. They hear language during almost every waking moment. They are provided with continuous opportunities to hear oral language.

- The language they hear is totally uncensored. They hear full, whole, mature adult language from the start.

- Children are exposed to the widest range of content possible. They hear individuals speaking about families, shopping, mail, meals, housework, plumbing, history, homework, work, geography, current affairs, and the like. There are no restrictions on the content to which children are exposed.

- There is absolutely no demand for any response from children. It is clear to all adults that children need to hear the language for a substantial period of time prior to making any response whatsoever. The first rule of learning language is: All production is based on input! This simply means that in order to produce language, one must first be "filled up" with that language.

- When you speak to your children, you use a wide range of words even though you know that your children cannot possibly understand those words. In the initial stage of language learning, adults provide children with the full range of language. Children come into this world with the ability to figure out all the rules of language. However, they must have full, mature, complex language upon which to operate. If you speak to children using only the words and grammar that you think they can understand, they will never fully develop complex oral language.

- During this stage, when you speak to your children, you might notice that you do not maintain eye contact with them throughout the interactions. Even if you want to gaze into their eyes, they will not allow you to maintain that eye contact for a long time. This is because at that early age, children are more interested in movement than in language interaction. Even so, they are still listening to language, and learning about language.

The ear is doing the work for language development at this time. Even though the eyes seem disinterested, the ear is continuously at work figuring out the rules of language.

In review then, the characteristics of the languaging to stage are:
- continuous immersion
- no demand for response
- children are exposed to complex, uncensored language
- wide range of content
- children do not have to understand everything they hear
- children do not have to be looking directly at you

Language Done With Children

The languaging to stage is the priority for nine to eighteen months, depending on the child. It assumes a different level of importance when children utter their first words. This somehow tells adults that the system is "ready" and children will now begin to produce. Our entire interactional patterns change. We automatically switch our emphasis to stage two, the languaging with stage. The rules of interaction are now quite different. The characteristics of stage two are discussed below.

- **Expectation of response**

  We now expect and sometimes demand a response from children. We expose children to a word and strongly encourage them to say the word. (For example, " jacket..say jacket honey, jacket, jacket.") We badger children to say words for friends and relatives. We expect them to respond. We even call friends on the phone just to have them hear our children speak.

- **Interaction**

  Because we now expect a response, there is a lot of interaction during this stage. When we talk to children, we make an effort to establish and maintain eye contact. Children are now more willing to look at speakers because language is becoming a much more interesting and important stimulus.

- **Narrower range of content**

  During this stage, the range of content does narrow significantly. We now realize that children are becoming able to repeat what they hear. We begin to watch what we say to them. In addition, we know that they are beginning to focus on learning language, so we speak to them more slowly, using words that we think they will understand. Although we still practice stage one language behavior, we predominantly use stage two interactions when we are speaking directly to children.

- **Modeling**

  A major characteristic of stage two is modeling. We tend to demonstrate language often for our children. We show them how the language works and help them to produce and to develop their own language. We verbally label things or make comments and encourage children to repeat them. We operate under an " I'll do it—now you do it" model. We tirelessly model language for our children.

- **Repetition**

  A hallmark of stage two is repetition. We continuously repeat words, phrases, comments and information for children. Somehow, we intuitively know that they need this repeated input in order to learn.

- **Predictable content**

  Because adults repeat language so much, it becomes very predictable for children. They know that in the morning, certain phrases will always be used. There is mealtime language, bathtime language, bedtime language, dressing time language, shopping language, play language and the like. There are highly predictable contexts in which language occurs. Predictability happens because children hear the same types of language repeated often within specific contexts. Predictability helps children to learn language easily and quickly.

- **Helping**

  In stage two, adults are bent on helping children learn to speak. They repeat language and support learning by complimenting and reinforcing children when they produce. They respond to all attempts to use language, provide much praise and reinforcement, do not expect perfection and are not critical of children's efforts.

It is important to recognize that languaging to children does not stop. It continues. However, modeling now has the priority.

In review then, the characteristics of the languaging with stage are :

- interaction
- demand for response
- narrower range of content
- modeling
- helping
- repetition
- predictable content

Language Done By Children

The languaging with stage continues until about ages four or five, at which point, children "own" language for themselves. Adults certainly continue to language to and with children, but the nature of the interactions are quite different. The interactions are different because children are now different. They direct their own conversations, select their own topics, make substantial contributions to interactions and master many complex grammatical forms. They listen to speakers and make meaningful responses. They question and create answers. They come into their own with language and demonstrate their competence. They become independent with language. They perform language by themselves. The important thing to remember about stage three is this: The quality of language production in stage three is directly related to the quality of language input and interaction children receive in stages one and two. It is not possible to have quality production without providing quality input.

These three language learning stages of to, with and by explain the process of language development. We will see in the next chapter that the same stages need to be duplicated in the development of reading. They hold the keys to the creation of a literate environment for children.

PERSONAL RECORD

- WHAT I REMEMBER MOST ABOUT MY CHILDREN'S LANGUAGING TO STAGES

_____

_____

_____

_____

_____

_____

_____

_____

_____

_____

- WHAT I REMEMBER MOST ABOUT MY CHILDREN'S LANGUAGING WITH STAGES

_____

_____

_____

_____

_____

_____

_____

_____

_____

_____

NEW INSIGHTS, INTERESTING OBSERVATIONS AND GOALS
RELATED TO LANGUAGING TO, WITH AND BY

Insights

_____

_____

_____

_____

_____

_____

Observations

_____

_____

_____

_____

_____

_____

Goals

_____

_____

_____

_____

_____

_____

3 READING : AN OLD FRIEND IN A NEW FORM

In the last chapter, we discussed the natural way in which oral language develops. We saw that there is a very specific environment in which language develops. This environment begins with immersion in natural language, moves to continuous modeling by mature language users, and ends with independence in language performance. This process allows oral language to be developed without any direct instruction or specific skills. If we look closely at the process of oral language development, what we will see is a useful blueprint for reading development. The secret rests in the simple and familiar concepts of to, with and by. At the beginning of this book, we learned that humans do four things with language. We listen to it, we speak it, we read it and we write it. These four acts, listening, speaking, reading and writing are referred to in educational circles as the language arts. The first two, listening and speaking, are species specific in that we are born to do them. They are primary language abilities. The second two, reading and writing, are human inventions and have to be learned within the environment. However, because they are based on primary oral language, they are extremely closely related to listening and speaking. It follows then that if there is a close relationship between the development of the primary language skill of speaking and the secondary language skills of reading and writing, then the process of learning reading and writing may be similar to that of learning speaking . Herein lies the key! If you learn and believe nothing more that is presented in this book, please learn, believe and remember this:

Reading and writing can develop in children in a natural and easy manner if we as adults create home and school environments based on the blueprint for oral language development. Let us review this blueprint.

First, there must be immersion. This means that the environment should continuously reflect print. There should be a lot of print in the home and at school. The print should be interesting, meaningful and child based. Children should see adults reading print every day. The most important aspect of the environment, however, is that children should be read to daily. As we read to children, we need to remember the characteristics of this stage. These will be reviewed in the next chapter. This period should begin at birth and continue indefinitely. However, it should be the priority from birth to approximately ages three to four.

Second, there must be modeling. This means that once children respond to specific words and phrases, adults need to switch priorities. This does not ever mean that reading to children stops. It simply means that reading with children becomes a daily experience. The type of print now changes to reflect more repetition, predictability and familiarity. We read books over and over again. We have children echo us (repeat small segments after us) or read along with us. We interact a great deal with children and we provide many opportunities to practice what they already know. We give children a lot of positive feedback for their efforts and we reward them for learning. This stage continues through the second or third grade or as long as it takes children to become independent in reading.

Third is the by stage in which children gain independence. In this stage, they can read by themselves and have a clear understanding of material on their reading level. This is the goal of literacy. However, the road to literacy is made significantly more tedious if the first two stages have not been experienced at home. Our task as parents and teachers is to embark upon the magnificent journey into literacy with our children. This journey will require great commitment to creating an environment that will support literacy. It is a very attainable goal. Every individual parent and teacher can transform any home or classroom setting into a dynamic, enjoyable, literate environment. The following chapters will clearly outline the steps that we can take to guide us on our journey into literacy.

4 READING TO CHILDREN

Reading to children is surely the most important contributor to literacy development. It serves some very critical purposes:

- It provides wonderful bonding between adults and children. As you hold your children on your lap or your knee, have them close to you, and share the wonders of print with them, you create some special and memorable moments.
- It exposes them to the sheer joy of print.
- It helps them to recognize that print holds the answers to many of their questions.
- It establishes a value for learning in general and reading in particular.
- It familiarizes them with the language of print which is quite different from that of oral language.
- It introduces them to the conventions of print.
  For example, print moves from top to bottom, from left to right and there are spaces between each word.
- It familiarizes them with the traditions of print such as capitalization and punctuation.
- It provides them with the opportunity to start learning meaningful words and phrases.
- It provides them with information which will have a positive impact on comprehension.
- It exposes them to new vocabulary.
- It provides good models of oral reading.
- It shows them how to behave when they meet unknown words or when they make mistakes.

It is recommended that you read to your children twice a day for approximately 20 to 30 minutes in each time block. Remember that literacy development represents a value, and that establishing a value takes time. If you want your children to become expert swimmers, or dancers or ball players, you would never miss a practice. You would arrange your schedule around that activity and it would be a priority. Literacy development must be thought of with the same degree of passion. You must be clearly committed to it and make it a priority.

The morning reading session would best be devoted to the reading of factual, content material such as science, geography, how things work, people, animals, current events and the like. This type of reading works best in the morning because such content is more difficult to process and to understand, and requires more concentration and effort. Children are more alert and willing to focus when they are rested and fresh.

The evening session may be devoted to the reading of stories, fables, poems, songs, rhymes, riddles, fairy tales and the like.

Purposes

There are several purposes or reasons for reading to young children. It is very important that you know these reasons so that you can vary the purposes of your reading often. The reason for reading will directly affect the way in which you read. This section will discuss these purposes and methods of reading and will suggest appropriate materials.

Purpose # 1
To introduce children to the joy, stimulation and rewards of print

Methods
- Begin reading for this purpose when your infants are approximately three months old. Continue through the elementary grades and beyond.
- Your older children may be looking at the pictures occasionally, coloring, eating, painting, getting ready for bed, playing quietly or resting on your lap.
- Your children need not be seated beside you or be totally attentive.

When you read for this purpose, the important thing is that the print comes in through the ear and not necessarily through the eye. Do not be discouraged if your very young children show no interest in looking at the book or at the pictures. Keep on reading because the valuable information is being absorbed through the ear. The eye connection will come later.

- Do not feel compelled to ask a lot of questions or to hold children accountable for the content read. Answer all questions. If you need to, ask very nonspecific questions such as, "Did you like the story? What was your favorite part? Who was your favorite character? Which was your favorite page?" Also, share your favorite characters and parts with them. This modeling is essential.
- Read with expression and passion. You are creating an advertisement for literacy for your children.

Materials

Following are some wonderful books that are ideal for reading for purpose #1. Continue to add other titles as you come across them. The basic rule for choosing books is choose those that you love. Reading is much better caught than taught. The more you love the selections you read, the more your children will catch the spirit.

Cloudy by Deborah King (Philomel, 1989)

Amazing Grace by Mary Hoffman (Dial Books, 1991)

Whistle For Willie by Ezra Jack Keats (Puffin Books, 1985)

Corduroy by Don Freeman (Viking Press, 1968)

Good Night Moon by Margaret Wise Brown (Harper and Row, 1975)

Benjy's Dog House by Margaret Bloy Grahm (Scholastic, 1973)

Bedtime For Francis by Russel Hoban (Harper and Row, 1960)

Teddy's Ear by Niki Daly (Viking Kestrell, 1985)

I Love You As Much by Laura Krauss Melmed (Lothrop, Lee and Shephard, 1993)

Tucking Mommy In by Morag Loh (Orchard Books, 1991)

On Mother's Lap by Ann Herbert Scott (Clarion, 1992)

Night Noises by Mem Fox (Harcourt, 1989)

This Quiet Lady by Charlotte Zolotow (Greenwillow, 1992)

Mamma, If You Had A Wish by Jeanne Modesitt (Green Tiger Press: Simon and Schuster, 1993)

Who Is The Beast? by Keith Baker (Harcourt, 1990)

Coat Of Many Colors by Dolly Parton (Harper Collins, 1994)

Angela's Wings by Jon Nones (Farrar, 1995)

A Window Of Time by Audrey Leighton (NADJA Publishing, 1995)

Amelia's Fantastic Flight by Rose Bursik (Henry Holt, 1992)

What You Know First by Patricia McLachlan (Joanna Cotler Books, 1995)

Stellaluna by Janell Cannon (Harcourt, 1993)

Grandfather Twilight by Barbara Berger (Philomel, 1984)

The Caterpillar And The Polliwog by Jack Kent (Simon and Schuster, 1982)

Where Does The Trail Lead? by Burton Albert (Simon and Schuster, 1991)

Here Is The Southwestern Desert by Madeline Dunphy (Hyperion Books, 1995)

The Three Little Javelinas by Susan Lowell (Northland, 1992)*

Night Tree by Eve Bunting (Harcourt, 1991)*

Mother Goose by Michael Hague (Holt, Rinehart and Winston, 1984)

Aunt Flossie's Hats by Elizabeth Fitzgerald Howard (Clarion Books, 1991)*

The Wednesday Surprise by Eve Bunting (Clarion Books, 1989)*

*identifies longer, more sophisticated selections

The Stolen Egg by Sue Vyner (Viking Press, 1992)

The Mare On The Hill by Thomas Locker (Dial Books, 1985)

Fox's Dream by Tejima (Philomel Books, 1985)

Bringing The Rain To Kapiti Plain by Verna Aardema (Dial Books, 1981)

An Enchanted Hair Tale by Alexis De Veaux (Harper Trophy Books, 1991)*

Owl Moon by Jane Yolen (Philomel Books, 1987)*

Papa, Please Get The Moon For Me by Eric Carle (Picture Book Studio U.S.A., 1986)

Daniel's Dog by Jo Ellen Bogart (Scholastic, 1990)

Bright Eyes, Brown Skin by Cheryl Willis Hudson (Scholastic, 1990)

Salt Hands by Jane Aragon (E.P. Dutton, 1989)

Mupharo's Beautiful Daughters by John Steptoe (Scholastic, 1987)*

Knots On A Counting Rope by Bill Martin Junior and John Archambault (The Trumpet Club, Bantam Doubleday Dell, 1987)

More Than Anything Else by Marie Bradby (*Orchard, 1995)

Following is a list of favorite story, touch and feel and cloth books for very young (birth to age 2) children.

Just A Snowy Day by Mercer Mayer (Golden Books, 1983)

Pokey Little Puppy's Day At The Fair (Golden Books, 1990)

Cindy Szekere's Good Night Sweet Mouse (Golden Books, 1988)

Pat The Bunny by Dorothy Kunhardt (Golden Books, 1984)

Pat The Cat by Edith Kunhardt (Golden Books, 1984)

Kitty Whiskers by Susan T. Hall (Golden Books, 1991)

The Touch Me Book (Golden Books, 1991)

Night Sounds, Morning Colors by Rosemary Wells, (Dial Books, 1994)

*identifies longer, more sophisticated selections

Baby's Favorite Things (Random House, 1986)

Kite In The Park by Lucy Cousins (Candlewick Press, 1992)

Flower In The Garden by Lucy Cousins (Candlewick Press, 1992)

Elmo Wants A Bath (Random House, 1992)

Teddy In The House by Lucy Cousins (Candlewick Press, 1992)

Bunny Rattle (Random House, 1989)

Let's Go To The Petting Zoo With Jungle Jack (Doubleday, 1992)

As you find books on this list that you really like, feel free to place a check beside those selections to remember them. Remember that this book is a workbook to be used to help you in your creation of a literate environment for your children.

Please do not get discouraged at the number of recommended books. It is not necessary to own all these books. If you have access to a library, please use it often. Borrow the books, then buy only those you and your children really like. If your library does not have a title you wish to see, feel free to recommend it to your librarian.

Once you decide to own specific books, then provide relatives and family friends a list of books that may be given for birthdays, Christmas and other special occasions. Also, organize book trades or book loans with close friends that have children of relatively the same ages as yours. It is not necessary to own hundreds of books to have a very literate environment.

PERSONAL RECORD

Additional Titles, New Insights, Interesting Observations

_____

_____

_____

_____

_____

_____

_____

_____

_____

_____

_____

_____

_____

_____

_____

_____

_____

_____

_____

_____

_____

_____

_____

_____

Purpose #2
To introduce children to new concepts

This is a very important purpose indeed. Concepts form the basis of comprehension. The more concepts your children have, the greater their chance at comprehending information when they go to school. When you read to children to develop new concepts, it is important that you are aware of the following guidelines:

Methods
- Seat children beside you.
- Have children look at the book if it has pictures.
- Read the entire book or selectionwithout stopping, then go back to the beginning, reread and stop often to discuss.
- Repeat complex or important segments a few times.
- Read more slowly so that children absorb the material.
- Read shorter segments at a time, then discuss what you have read.
- Always check for comprehension by asking them to explain the concepts you have discussed.
- Encourage children to respond. If they can't, then you immediately model ("I asked you ———. I think that the answer is ———. I think that because ———.")
- Read concept books over and over throughout several weeks.
- Interact with your children.

Materials
Following are some ideal books for conceptual development. Again, feel free to add to the list at any time.

My First Book Of Shapes
My First Book Of Words
My First Book Of Colors
My First Book Of Numbers
All by Eric Carle (Thomas Crowell, 1974)

Big Ones, Little Ones by Tana Hoban (William Morrow, 1976)

My First Number Book by Marie Heinst (Darlig Kindersley Inc., 1992)

One Yellow Lion by Matthew Van Fleet (Dial Books, 1992)

My First Look At.....Series (Random House, 1991)
Titles include:

Time	**Opposites**
Numbers	**Things That Go**
Colors	**Noises**
Sorting	**Home**
Shopping	**Nature**

Seven Blind Mice by Ed Young (Philomel Books, 1992)

Alphabet Books

Animalia by Graeme Base (Harry N. Abrams Inc., 1986)

A Was Once An Apple Pie by Julie Lacome (Candlewick Press, 1992)

The Monster Book Of A B C Sounds by Alan Snow (Dial Books, 1991)

The A B C Bunny by Wanda Gag (Coward McCann, 1933)

The Handmade Alphabet by Laura Rankin (Sign Language) (Dial Books, 1991)

A Is For Angry by Sandra Boynton (Workman Publishers, 1987)

Anno's Alphabet by Anno (Harper Trophy/Harper and Row, 1975)

Alphabet Puzzle by Jill Downie (Lothrop, 1988)

C Is For Colorado by Gayle Corbett Shirley (ABC Press, 1989)

PERSONAL RECORD
Additional Titles, New Insights, Interesting Observations

_____

_____

_____

_____

_____

_____

_____

_____

_____

_____

_____

_____

_____

_____

_____

_____

_____

_____

_____

_____

_____

_____

Purpose# 3

To sensitize children to their own feelings and to the feelings of others

Methods

- Children do not have to be looking at the book.
- Children need to be attentive and to listen as you read.
- Ask how your children feel about emotional parts.
- Ask children to identify how characters feel.
- Share your own feelings with your children.
- Reinforce the idea that it is good to feel, even though it may hurt a bit. Let children know that you too cry when you read certain books. It is important that children know that "feeling" is a good thing.
- Ask questions such as :

  How does (a certain event) make you feel?

  How do you think (a character) felt when ————?

  How would you feel if ————?

  How can you tell that ———— feels ————?

  Why does (a character) feel————?

  How do you think ————would feel if————?

  How would you help————feel better?

  Remember to **model** when children cannot answer!

Materials

Following is a list of some excellent books that tap deep and important emotions. Again, please add your own personal titles and share them with your children.

Everett Anderson's Goodbye by Lucille Clifton (death) (The Trumpet Club, 1983)

A Rose For Abby by Donna Guthrie (compassion for the homeless) (Abingdon Press, 1988)

Darkness And The Butterfly by Ann Grifalconi (fear of darkness) (Little, Brown and Co., 1987)

Daniel's Dog by Jo Ellen Bogart (jealousy of a new sibling) (Scholastic, 1990)

Through Grandpa's Eyes by Patricia MacLachlan (learning from a blind granfather) (Harper Trophy Books, 1980)

Let The Celebrations Begin by Margeret Wild and Julie Vivas (liberation from a German concentration camp) (Orchard Books, 1991)

Love You Forever by Robert Munsch (aging parent) (Firefly Books, 1989)

The Wall by Eve Bunting (war) (Clarion Books, 1990)

Wilfrid Gordon McDonald Partridge by Mem Fox (befriending the aged) (Kane Miller Books, 1984)

Amazing Grace by Mary Hoffman (overcoming being different) (Dial Books, 1991)

The Two Of Them by Aliki (death of a grandparent) (Mulberry Books, 1979)

The Fourth Good Thing About Barney by Judith Viorst (death of a pet) (Atheneum, 1971)

Daddy And Me by Jeanne Moutoussamy—Ashe (aids) (Knopf, 1993)

Only Opal by Barbara Cooney (being an orphan) (Philomel, 1994)

Grandad Bill's Song by Jane Yolen (death of a grandparent) (Philomel, 1994)

Cheyenne Again by Eve Bunting (being different) (Clarion, 1995)

Grandma According To Me by Karen Magnuson Beil (relationships) (Dell, 1992)

All Those Secrets Of The World by Jane Yolen (friendship) (Little, Brown, 1991)

PERSONAL RECORD
Additional Titles, New Insights, Interesting Observations

_____

_____

_____

_____

_____

_____

_____

_____

_____

_____

_____

_____

_____

_____

_____

_____

_____

_____

_____

_____

_____

_____

_____

_____

_____

Purpose#4
To develop children's sense of humor

This is a very important reason for reading to children. Humor is called a metalinguistic skill. This means that in order to appreciate humor, one has to almost stand away from language, observe it objectively and "get" it. Prior to age 2 or 2 &1/2, children have few metalinguistic skills. They tend to laugh at what they do not understand. As they grow older, however, those skills develop and they are ready to expand their humor. By age three, most children become increasingly able to deal with humor.

Methods
When you read for this purpose, there are few rules:
- Read with much passion, expression and involvement.
- ENJOY yourself!
- Share what you find funny with the children.
- Ask about what is funny to your children.

Materials
The Wolf's Chicken Stew by Keiko Kasza (G.P. Putnams's Sons, 1987)

Imogene's Antlers by David Small (Crown Publishers, 1985)

Are You My Mother? by P. D. Eastman (Random House, 1960)

Horton Hatches An Egg by Dr. Seuss (Random House, 1940)

Rain Makes Applesauce by Julian Sheer (Holiday House, 1964)

Silly Questions and Funny Answers by William Wiesner (Scholastic, 1974)

My Grandpa Henry by Barbara Swaby (Current Inc., Colorado Springs, CO.1993)

A Chocolate Moose For Dinner by Fred Gwynne (Trumpet Club, 1976)

Math Curse by Jon Scieszka and Lane Smith (Viking, 1995)

PERSONAL RECORD
Additional Titles, New Insights, Interesting Observations

_____

_____

_____

_____

_____

_____

_____

_____

_____

_____

_____

_____

_____

_____

_____

_____

_____

_____

_____

_____

_____

_____

_____

_____

_____

Purpose # 5
To introduce children to a variety of great art work

Literacy certainly involves the ability to read well on skill and comprehension levels. In addition to the skills of reading, however, is an aesthetic or artistic appreciation that is essential to real reading. It is very important that this artistic love begins at home and is nurtured and fostered at school. This purpose should be a continuous part of your early reading experiences with your children. Some children are ready for this type of reading as early as two years old. For most, three years old is an ideal time to start.

Methods
When you read for this purpose, here are some suggestions:
• Have children beside you so that they can see the book.
• Read the story first, then go back and enjoy the artwork.
• Talk about the art and identify the type of art work. (pen and ink, water color, pencil sketches, markers, photographs, realistic art, impressionistic art, abstract art, etc.)
• Compare art from different books. Have children react to each.
• Be sensitive to the artistic preferences of children.
• Ask children about likes and dislikes.
• Share your artistic biases with your children.
• Encourage children to create their own illustrations for their favorite books. Help them to try different art media.

Materials
Each year in the United States, one book is selected, based on its outstanding artwork, to receive the Caldecott Award. These books are of superior artistic quality. Please expose your children to as many of them as you can. These books are worth reading and enjoying over and over again. Following is a list of the Caldecott Award Winners for the past twenty five years. A list of winners from 1950 is easily found at your local library.

1966   *Always Room For One More* by Sorche McLeodhas (Holt)

1967   *Sam, Bangs and Moonshine* by Evaline Ness (Holt)

1968   *Drummer Hoff* by Barbara Emberley (Prentice Hall)

1969   *The Fool Of The World And The Flying Ship* by Arthur Ransome (Farrar)

1970   *Sylvester And The Magic Pebble* by William Steig (Windmill Press)

1971   *A Story, A Story* by Gail Haley (Atheneum)

1972   *One Fine Day* by Nonny Hogrogian (Macmillan)

1973   *The Funny Little Woman* by Arlene Mosel (Dutton)

1974   *Duffy And The Devil* by Harve Zemach (Farrar)

1975   *Arrow To The Sun* by Gerald McDermott (Viking Press)

1976   *Why Mosquitoes Buzz In People's Ears* by Verna Aardema (Dillon Press)

1977   *Ashanti To Zulu: African Traditions* by Margaret Musgrove (Dial Press)

1978   *Noah's Ark* by Peter Spier (Doubleday)

1979   *The Girl Who Loved Wild Horses* by Paul Goble (Bradbury)

1980   *Ox-Cart Man* by Donald Hall (Viking Press)

1981   *Fables* by Arnold Lobel (Harper and Row)

1982   *Jumanji* by Chris Van Allsburg (Houghton Mifflin)

1983   *Shadow* by Blaise Cendrars (Scribner's)

1984   *The Glorious Flight* by Marsha Brown (Scribner's)

1985   *St. George And The Dragon* by Margaret Hodges (Little, Brown and Co.)

1986   *The Polar Express* by Chris Van Allsburg (Farrar)

1987   *Hey, Al!* by Arthur Yorinks (Farrar)

1988   *Owl Moon* by Jane Yolen (Philomel)

1989   *Song And Dance Man* by Karen Ackerman (Knoph)

1990   *Lon Po Po* by Ed Young (Philomel)

1991   *Black And White* by David Macaulay (Houghton Mifflin)

1992   *Tuesday* by David Wiesner (Clarion Books)

1993   *Mirette On The High Wire* by Emily Arnold McCully (Putnam)

1994   *Grandfather's Journey* by Allen Say (Houghton Mifflin)

1995   *Smoky Night* by Eve Bunting (Harcourt)

1996   *Officer Buckle and Gloria* by Peggy Rathmann (Putnam)

1997   *Golem* by David Wiesniewski (Clarion)

1998   *Rapunzel* by Paul O. Zelinsky

1999   *Snowflake Bentley* by Jacqueline Briggs-Martin (Houghton Mifflin)

2000   *Joseph Had A Little Overcoat* by Simms Taback (Viking)

2001   *So You Want To Be President?* by Judith St. George (Philomel)

2002   *The Three Pigs* by David Wiesner (Clarion Books)

2003   *My Friend Rabbit* by Eric Rohmann (Roaring Book Press/ Millbrook Press)

2004 ***The Man Who Walked Between The Towers*** by Mordicai Gerstein (Roaring Book Press/Millbrook Press)

2005 ***Kitten's First Full Moon*** by Kevin Henkes (Greenwillow Books/Harper Collins Publishers)

In addition to the Caldecott winners, there are so many books with wonderful artwork for children. A few of those follow:

Aida by Leontyne Price (Harcourt, Brace and Jovanovich, 1990)

Cloudy by Deborah King (Philomel Books, 1989)

Animalia by Graeme Base (Harry N. Abrams, 1986)

The Mare On The Hill by Thomas Locker (Dial Books, 1985)

The Great Kapok Tree by Lynne Cherry (Harcourt, Brace and Jovanovich, 1990)

Fox's Dream by Tejima (Philomel, 1985)

This Quiet Lady by Charlotte Zolotow (Greenwillow Books, 1992)

Aunt Flossie's Hats by Elizabeth Fitzgerald Howard (Clarion Books, 1991)

Brother Eagle, Sister Sky by Susan Jeffers (Dial Books, 1991)

Reflections by Ann Jonas (Greenwillow Books, 1987)

Mufaro's Beautiful Daughters by John Steptow (Scholastic, 1987)

Salt Hands by Chelsea Aragon (E. P. Dutton, 1989)

The Mitten by Jan Brett (Putnam, 1989)

Giving Thanks by Chief Jake Swamb (Lee and Low, 1995)

PERSONAL RECORD
Additional Titles, New Insights, Interesting Observations

_____

_____

_____

_____

_____

_____

_____

_____

_____

_____

_____

_____

_____

_____

_____

_____

_____

_____

_____

_____

_____

_____

Purpose # 6
To provide children with real life information

This is a critical reason for reading to children. It literally helps to form the base for comprehension both in and out of school. If, for example, your children are taught about coral reefs in the third grade, their exposure to coral reefs in your reading to them will certainly help them to comprehend the information more easily at that time. This is because comprehension is based on prior knowledge (the information that we already know). Our task then, as adults who are responsible for children, is to expand and deepen their prior knowledge banks continuously, so as to enhance, and to a great extent ensure comprehension.

This purpose for reading requires specific methods.

Following are important suggestions.

Methods
- Start reading for this purpose when children are approximately three years old. However, some children are ready for content reading at two years old. Observe your children! If they have long attention spans, are wanting to know and choose content material to be read to them; go for it!
- Your children must listen carefully.
- Children ought not to be engaged in any other activity such as drawing, painting etc.
- If there are pictures that illustrate the facts you are presenting, children should look at them.
- Please read the selections at least two or three times at one sitting and repeat them over several weeks or months depending on the complexity of the material and the learning rate of your children. It is so important to note that it takes the average learner approximately seventy repetitions of information to learn it to an automatic level. Children with learning problems require even more repetitions. One of the most valu-

able keys to literacy is continuous and repeated input over **a long period of time.**

• As you read, encourage your children to visualize or make pictures of the information in their heads. The more they learn to visualize, the better their comprehension will be.

• Read short segments then check for comprehension by asking questions. Before they answer, remind them to check their pictures .

• When they answer incorrectly, reread appropriate segments and encourage visualization.

• Model responses for your children.

• Discuss the information with your children.

Materials (**Good for preschool age as well as older children**)
The Sun, The Wind and The Rain by Lisa Westberg Peters (Henry Holt and Co., 1988)

Hey! Get Off Our Train by John Burmingham (endangered species) (Crown Publishers, 1989)

Big, Bigger, Biggest by Kate Banks (Alfred Knopf, 1990)

The Rock Pool by David Bellamy (Clarkson N. Potter Inc., 1988)

The King Who Rained by Fred Gwynne (Windmill Books, Simon and Schuster, 1978)

A Cache of Jewels by Ruth Heller (Grosset and Dunlap, 1987)

The Great Kapok Tree by Lynne Cherry (Harcourt Brace and Jovanovich, 1990)

My Very First Learn and Know Question and Answer Book by Brenda Apsley (Preschool Press, Playmore Inc., Waldman Publishing Corp. 1986)

Antarctica by Helen Cowcher (Farrar, 1990)

Visiting The Art Museum by Laurene Krasny Brown and Marc Brown (E. P. Dutton, 1986)

Dolphins by Margaret Davidson (Scholastic, 1964)

Ashanti to Zulu: African Traditions by Margaret Musgrove (Dial Books, 1976)

My First Book About Space by Dinah L. Moche (Golden Books, 1982)

Fish Do The Strangest Things by Leonora and Arthur Hornblow (Step Up Books, Random House, 1966)

The Big Little Golden Book Of Planets (Golden Books, 1987)

Dinosaurs Of The Land, Sea and Air (Modern Publishing, A Division of Unisystems, 1988)

Dinosaurs and Prehistoric Creatures (Modern Publishing, Unisystems, 1988)

The Big Book Of Questions And Answers (Publications International, Ltd., 1989)

Dinosaurs: A Lost World: A Pop Up Book by Keith Moseley and Robert Cremins (G. P. Putnam's Sons, 1984)

Dinosaurs (Random House, 1977)

Hear Your Heart by Paul Showers (Thomas Crowell, 1968)

Dinosaur Hunters by Kate McMullan (Houghton Mifflin, 1991)

Thinking: A Troll Question Book by Kathie Billingslea Smith and Victoria Crenson (Troll Associates, 1988)

Birds by Peter Gill (Troll Associates, 1990)

Animal Close-Ups Series (Charlesbridge Publishers, 1989)
Titles include:

The Cheetah	***The Penguin***
The Elephant	***The Seal***

Creepy Crawlies by Ruth Thompson (Aladin Books, 1990)

See How They Grow Series (Lodestar Gooks, Dutton, 1991)
Titles include:

Frog	***Duck***
Kitten	***Puppy***

Baby Animals: True Stories by Dereck Hall (Candlewick Press, 1989)

(These titles are good for children ages 5 and up)

Pablo Picasso by Ibi Lepscky (Trumpet Club, 1984

Dinosaur Mysteries by Mary Elting and Ann Goodman (Platt and Munk, Publishers, 1980)

The Glow In The Dark Night Sky Book by Clint Hatchett (Random House, 1988)

Giants Of Land and Air: Past And Present by David Peters (A Sierra Club Book, Alfred A. Knopf, 1986)

Looking At Insects by David Suzuki (Stoddart Publishing, Canada, 1986)

Picture Encyclopedia Of The World For Children (Exeter Books, 1984)

The Golden Book Encyclopedia (Books A to Z) (Golden Books)

Childcraft Encyclopedia (World Book Inc., 1987)

Save Our Species Series (Tiger, Rhino, Gorilla, Panda) by Jill Bailey (Gallery Books, 1990)

Saving The Peregrine Falcon by Caroline Arnold (Houghton Mifflin, 1985)

The Magic School Bus Inside The Human Body
The Magic School Bus At The Waterworks
The Magic School Bus Inside The Earth
The Magic School Bus Lost In The Solar System
all by Joanna Cole (Scholastic, 1989 - 1990)

Sierra by Diane Siebert (Harper Collins Publishers, 1991)

Herds Of Words by Patricia MacCarthy (Dial, 1991)

Panther Dream: A Story Of The African Rain Forest by Bob and Wendy Weir (Hyperion Books For Children, 1991)

The Six Bridges Of Humphrey The Whale by Toni Knapp (The Rockrimmon Press Inc., Colorado Springs, CO., 1989)

Many Luscious Lolliopops: A Book About Adjectives by Ruth Heller (Sandcastle, 1989)

Up, Up and Away: A Book About Adverbs by Ruth Heller (Sandcastle, 1991)

Merry-Go-Round: A Book About Nouns by Ruth Heller (Sandcastle, 1990)

Somewhere Today by Bert Kitchen (Candlewick, 1992)

Math Curse by Jon Scieszka and Lane Smith (Viking, 1995)

What Good Is A Cactus? by Peter Marchand (Roberts Rinehart, 1994)

All The Colors Of The Earth by Sheila Hamanaka (Morrow, 1994)

PERSONAL RECORD
Additional Titles, New Insights, Interesting Observations

Purpose # 7
To develop children's vocabulary and comprehension

All of us as parents or teachers know the importance of helping our children comprehend information.

Comprehension is not really a reading matter. It affects all academic areas. As they enter school, children are expected to comprehend all material that is presented to them. Throughout this book, the importance of comprehension has been stressed. This is a critical purpose of reading to children. We have already discussed filling up children's prior knowledge banks by reading them informational books. This segment has to do with the fostering of comprehension by developing vocabulary, thinking skills and visualization.

Methods
- Children should be attentive and listen.
- Read the entire book through, then reread, stopping to discuss important or interesting words.
- Ask questions such as:
  What does this word mean?
  What word on this page means ————?
  What word tells you that————?
  What word let us know that ————?
  Why do you think the author used the word——?
  What is another word that means the same as____?
- Have children choose their favorite words and keep a collection of them on slips of paper or on note cards in a "Favorite Word Box."
- As you read, identify one or two really important and interesting words to teach children. The teaching of words should include the following steps:
  Identify the CLASS to which the word belongs; the PROPERTIES of the word or what the word has or does to make it special; the RELATED

WORDS, or words that children already know that are similar in meaning to the new word; and an EXAMPLE of the word.

Example: The new word is **timid**.

CLASS: " Timid is an emotion or a feeling."

PROPERTIES: " When you are timid, you feel shy and nervous, you feel that people are staring at you or laughing at you, your stomach feels sick sometimes, sometimes your hands shake, you often wish you were at home, alone, with your parents."

RELATED WORDS: "The word timid is kind of like shy and afraid, but it feels more scary.

EXAMPLE: " Remember last month when your preschool teacher wanted you to share your poem with the class and you started to cry and wouldn't say it at all? You cried because you were timid. Can you remember another time when you were timid?"

Notice how much information you have provided for children about the word. This helps children to really understand and remember words.

- After you have presented the words, use them liberally in your conversations with your children. Children will learn words that they hear often in their environments.
- Talk about what you have read. First, remember to encourage children to make pictures of what they hear. Visualization is the key to remembering literal information. Have them check their pictures before they answer. For example, "As you listen to the story, use your brain as a camera and make pictures of what you hear."
- Ask children a variety of questions. Normally, when we ask children questions about what we read, we tend to ask literal questions such as : Who.....? What.....? When......? and Where........? There is nothing wrong with these questions except that we ask too many of them. These ques-

tions require children to simply regurgitate information. In trying to facilitate comprehension, however, you need to expose children to a much wider range of questions that not only prompts memory, but actually trains and stimulates thinking. In addition to the literal questions, then, use questions such as the following:

What would happen if.....?

If you were............, how would you ....?

What might happen next?

How do you know that............?

What tells you that ....?

What would you think if............?

How would you feel if............?

How is ....like............?

How can you tell that...............?

Why did ....happen?

What is another way that (someone) could have ....?

Why did..........behave in this way?

What made.................say or do or think.........?

Remember to model thinking to your children if they cannot respond appropriately. To model, repeat the question, (Honey, I asked you how the bear in the story feels.) Answer the question, (I think he feels very sad.) Show where you found the answer, (Listen. the story says that a tear rolled down his face.) Show how you got from the book to your answer (I know that when a tear rolls down someone's face, it usually means that that person is sad. That is how I know that the bear is sad.) Modeling thinking is essential to the comprehension growth of children.

Materials

You may use just about any book to achieve this purpose. You also should expose young children to a variety of word books that focus on a specific set of words. A list of word books follows:

My First Book : Words And Pictures For The Very Young (Chadwick Press, 1992)

Richard Scary's Best Word Book Ever by Richard Scary (Golden Books, 1963)

Good Morning Words! (Scott Foresman, 1990)

My First Word Book by Angela Wilkies (Darlig Kindersley Inc., 1991)

500 Words To Grow On by Harry McNaught (Random House, 1973)

I Spy: A Book Of Pictures And Riddles by Walter Wick and Jean Marzollo (Scholastic, 1992)

What You Know First by Patricia MacLachlan (Cotler, 1995)

Water Dance by Thomas Locker (Harcourt, Brace, 1997)

PERSONAL RECORD

Additional Titles, New Insights, Interesting Observations

5 READING (TO AND) WITH CHILDREN

Daily reading will pay off! As you read to children year after year, you will observe them passing through four clearly identifiable stages. Stage one is **passive listening**. In this stage, children seem to listen passively to print. There seems to be no real connection with print and little response to the reading. Do not be discouraged. Remember that language requires time to make an impression on children. They often need time to just listen before they produce.

Stage two is **active listening**. In this stage, children begin to become involved in the reading sessions. They may ask questions about the material, seek clarification, make comments, voice opinions, request favorite books and the like. They are obviously involved with print in spite of the fact that they may not seem to attend to the written words themselves.

Stage three is **partial participation**. Here children begin to memorize material that they have heard repeatedly. They begin making comments and asking questions about print such as, "What does this word say? What is this word? Is this word ....? What does this word spell? Is this the same word that is on the other page? I know that word! I've seen that word before! I can find this word again!" They also begin to join in spontaneously as you read sections that they have memorized.

Stage four is **initial reading**. In this stage, children clearly begin to learn words by sight, to internalize phonic rules and to read familiar selections independently. They start to read unfamiliar signs and attempt to sound out simple words with some success. It is obvious that the process of real reading has begun.

Reading with children should begin in stage three. Many children, if they have been read to for a wide range of purposes from birth, move into this stage by age 3 or 3 and 1/2. For most children, age 4 seems to be an ideal time to begin the reading **with** stage. You need to remember the **characteristics** of languaging with children.

In review, they are:
- continuous interaction
- children need to respond
- narrower range of content
- much modeling
- direct and helpful feedback
- assistance whenever needed
- predictable content
- practice, practice, practice

As you enter the reading with stage, it is going to be necessary to rethink your reading sessions. Prior to this point, you have been reading to your children twice per day: once in the morning for factual content and once in the evening for narrative content. When you move into stage three, reading with needs to be the priority. This means that you will need to read with your children once every day. I suggest that you do your reading with every morning. During the evening period, you can continue your reading to times, alternating factual and narrative material (day 1 factual, day 2 narrative, day 3 factual, day 4 narrative, etc.) It is very important that once children enter the reading with stage, you support reading development every single day.

The major purpose of reading with children is to lead them naturally and easily into meaningful reading, alphabet recognition and identification, phonic analysis and word recognition. As you begin to read with children, it is very important that you are aware of and apply the following suggestions.

- Have children seated next to you so that they can see the book clearly.
- Read in a relatively noise free environment.
- Read in a place in which your children will experience minimal distractions.
- Read when your children are most rested and content.
- Read books over and over again! As children hear books many times, they begin to memorize them. Encourage this!

- As you read, run your finger slowly under the print you are reading, so that your children can begin to see the relationships that exist between what they hear and what they see on the page.
- Once children begin to memorize the books, begin to omit segments that they know, and encourage them to fill in the familiar words . Eg.
Love is a rainbow
Love is a smile
Love is a butterfly on a woodpile.
Your children may know the words...a *rainbow*, a *smile* and a *butterfly*..

Your reading would go like this:
Love is [stop reading, run your fingers under the next two words, and have your children say the words] *a rainbow*
(Adult) *Love is* (Children) *a smile*
(Adult) *Love is* (Children) *a butterfly*
(Adult) *on a woodpile.*

Let your children know that the words you are pointing to spell the words that they are saying.

Reinforce this every day!

- Use the **to, with, by** strategy often. Eg. Begin by reading a relatively short book that has almost been memorized. First, read the book to the children. Next, have the children read the book along with you. Finally, have children read the book by themselves. Provide as much assistance as needed.
- Read books that have **very** simple language and few words on each page. A list of easy reading books is provided at the end of this section.
- Read books that have very **predictable language patterns**. A list of these books is presented at the end of this section. It is important to read these books because they have clear patterns that lend themselves easily to memorization.
- Have children reread known books over and over again. Have them practice these books until they can read them fluently. Then have them tape the books and share them with peers, family members and family

friends. They may also use the tapes themselves to listen to at bedtime and the like.

- Once children have memorized specific words, copy those words on to small note cards. Help children to play games such as matching cards to words in books, identifying words on cards, playing concentration with duplicate cards and playing GO FISH with the cards.

- Keep the books that children have totally or partially memorized in one central place so that they are easily located. You will see that these books eventually become the reading by selections.

- As children begin to recognize words independently, create a word box in which to keep all the words they know. The word box can be a simple empty box, a pencil box, an empty can, a file box or any empty container. Reward them for learning X number of words.

- Begin to label many items in the environment. Start with children's bedrooms and use their names in the labels. (Dana's bed, Dana's chair, Dana's dresser) Print the labels on note cards. Use magic markers for clarity. Place the labels at children's eye level so that they can see them easily. Point to and talk about the labels often. Play games with labels. For example, remove two or three and have children replace them appropriately. As skill improves, remove more labels. Also, label items in other rooms.

- When you read in stage two, it is very important that you use the appropriate materials and that you provide enough practice. The booklists at the end of this section will be very helpful.

In review, the important things to do in the reading with stage are:
- read predictable print books over and over
- read easy reading books over and over
- start a word box or word bank.
- label items in the environment
- play games with words
- have children read with you

Getting Ready To Learn Phonics

Once you have established the reading with time and your children are learning words and memorizing books, it is a good time to begin to focus on introducing them to phonics. Remember that there is a big difference between teaching phonics and learning phonics. The purpose of this time is to help children learn phonics. First, let us discuss the meaning of phonics. Phonics has to do with knowledge of letters and the sounds represented by letters, blending sounds together, and internalizing the basic rules of word recognition. One of the greatest gifts parents can give to children is sending them to kindergarten knowing several words automatically, all the letter forms and the sounds of the letters. The key to learning the letters and sounds is continuous practice over a long period of time. In order to achieve this goal, parents need to begin alphabet work shortly after the reading with time has begun. This allows approximately eighteen months to two years to perfect the process. You can go slowly and relax if you do a little every day.

Alphabet Work

There are three important kinds of alphabet books. Each has specific purposes and helps to achieve different ends. The level one alphabet book introduces children to the concept of individual sounds. It identifies each letter and creates text that repeats the sound represented by that letter over and over for emphasis. The concept of the sound gets fixed in children's minds and begins to create a base for the understanding and memory of the sounds.
An example of level one text follows:

B Bully Benjamin

This is Benjamin. Benjamin is a handsome boy. He has bright blue eyes, bushy blonde hair and big beautiful dimples in his cheeks. Benjamin is also a brilliant boy. He is beginning first grade now, and believes that school is a breeze. This year, Benjamin's behavior is quite beyond reproach, but last year was a very different story. In kindergarten, Benjamin was known as the Big, Bad Bully.....believe it or not.

Notice the overkill on repeated use of words that start with the letter "b". This allows children to begin to internalize the concept of "B"ness. The goal is not to have children memorize anything, but to help them to conceptualize individual sounds. Children should be introduced to level one alphabet books in the reading to stage and at the start of the reading with stage.

The level two alphabet book provides children with short, easily memorized phrases or sentences that repeat single sounds often. The point of the phrases or sentences is to allow children to associate each letter with a series of pictures. This will lead them into learning letter/sound relationships. You will want to read these books to children often in the reading with stage in order to facilitate memorization. Discuss all the pictures associated with each letter with children.

An example of level two print follows.

P   Precious puppies proudly parading in the park.

(Discuss the puppies, how precious they are, the puppy parade and the park. Emphasize the /p/ sound slightly.)

Notice that the sentence is very short and extremely visual. That is the point. The sentence is created to help children form strong visual images which will foster memory. Choose your favorite one or two level two books and read them repeatedly in the reading with stage.

Level three alphabet books present children with one letter and only one related word and picture on each page. The point here is to help children anchor in their memory the relationship between each letter and its corresponding sound. This is where real letter/sound learning takes place. Choose one favorite level three alphabet book and focus on it throughout the reading with stage. Read it daily to children. Close the book, choose a letter, and have children visualize the picture that is on the page. Eg."Harry, can you tell me what is on the M page? Good job! M is for monkey." Read the entire book each day, then focus on practicing one or two pages with your children. Review the information at all convenient times such as driving in the car, at bathtime, at bedtime, as you fix meals, etc. You may also want to purchase an alphabet poster to use in your home.

An example of a level three book follows:

B

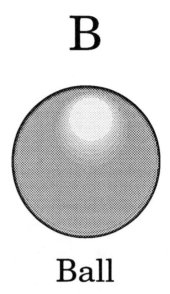

Ball

Once children can easily identify the letters and recall appropriate pictures, then it is time to move on. Help children to separate the individual sounds. For example, children can say: A is for Apple. Now move to: A is for Apple, /a/ /a/ /a/ (use the sound of "a") Apple. In this way children begin to learn the isolated sounds of each letter. Continue this activity until children can easily recall each letter and the accompanying sound (A=/a/, B=/b/, c=/c/ etc.) Remember that you have time to achieve this goal. Do not get in too much of a hurry. Do not be impatient. Remember To, With and By! If you begin early, you will have enough time to complete your journey into literacy with ease and joy.

You will need to reinforce letter sound learning continuously. One way to do this is to make **sound-concept tins**. These are tins or boxes that are wrapped or decorated and labeled with individual letters.

For example:

| B | | P |

In each tin or box, place many items that begin with specific letters. Have your children help to choose the items that go in each tin. Review a few of the tins each day.

As your children become more and more automatic at recalling letters and their sounds, play sound games with them. Some of these are:

Starts Like Game: Give children a word. Have them think of another word that has a similar beginning sound. If they cannot, model by providing a word. Continue until children are able to provide words without assistance.

Ends Like Game: Give children a word. Have them think of another word that has the same ending sound. Again, model if they cannot respond accurately. Please note that hearing ending sounds is a much more difficult skill than hearing beginning sounds. Do not begin this game before children are successful at the Starts Like Game.

Rhyming Game : Give children a word. Have them think of other words that rhyme. Again, model.

Materials

During the reading with time, you must have readily available a number of alphabet books, predictable print books and easy reading books which you have been reading and will continue to read over and over to your children. Following is a list of these books.

Alphabet Books
Level One
Aster Aardvark's Alphabet Adventures by Steven Kellogg (Morrow Junior Books, 1987)

Level Two
Animalia by Graeme Base (Harry A. Abrams, 1986)

A Was Once An Apple Pie by Julie Lacome (Candlewick Press, 1992)

The Monster Book Of ABC by Alan Snow (Dial Books, 1991)

The A B C Bunny by Wanda Gag (Coward McCann, 1961)

Level Three
The Handmade Alphabet by Laura Rankin (Dial Books, 1991)

A Is For Angry by Sandra Boynton (Workman Publishers, 1987)

Anno's Alphabet by Anno (Harper and Row, 1975)

On Market Street by Arnold Lobel (Mulberry Books, 1981)

Predictable Print Books
Brown Bear, Brown Bear, What Do You See? by Bill Martin Junior (Holt, Rinehart and Winston, 1967)

Young Joe by Jan Ormerod (Lothrop, Lee and Shepard, 1986)

The Very Hungry Caterpillar by Eric Carle (Philomel Books, 1981)

Pumpkin, Pumpkin by Jeanne Titherington (Greenwillow Books, 1986)

When I'm Sleepy by Jane Howard (E. P. Dutton, 1985)

The Napping House by Audrey Wood (Harcourt, Brace and Jovanovich, 1984)

If I Had by Mercer Mayer (Dial Press, 1968)

Goodbye, Hello by Robert Welber (Pantheon, 1974)

Love Is by Barbara Swaby (Current Inc., Colorado Springs, 1993)

My Grandpa Henry by Barbara Swaby (Current Inc., Colorado Springs, 1993)

Lisa Cannot Sleep by Kay Beckman (Franklin Watts, 1969)

Polar Bear, Polar Bear, What Do You Hear? by Bill Martin Junior and Eric Carle (Henry Holt and Company, 1991)

Here Are My Hands by Bill Martin Junior and John Archambault (Henry Holt and Company, 1985)

Good- Night Owl! by Pat Hutchins (Macmillan, 1972)

But Not The Hippopotamus by Sandra Boynton (Little Simon/ Simon and Schuster, 1982)

Are You My Mommy? A Pop Up Book by Carla Dijs (Simon and Schuster,1990)

Where's Mommy's Truck? by Harriet Ziefert and Andrea Baruffi (Harper Collins, 1992)

In A Dark, Dark Wood by David A. Carter (Simon and Schuster, 1991)

Pretend You're A Whale by Carla Dijs (Simon and Schuster, 1992)

Come Back Puppies and *Come Back Kittens* by Jan Ormerod (Lothrop, Lee and Shepard, 1992)

I Look Like This and *Look What I Found* by Nick Sharratt (Candlewick Press, 1992)

Ten Little Rabbits by Virginia Grossman and Sylvia Long (Chronicle Books, 1991)

Over In The Meadow by David Carter (Scholastic, 1992)

Fortunately by Remy Charlip (Trumpet Club, 1984)

Easy To Read Books
By Antoon Krings (Hyperion Books For Children, 1992)
Oliver's Strawberry Patch
Oliver's Bicycle
Oliver's Pool

Emily Wet The Bed by Domittille de Pressense (Checkerboard Press, 1990)

By Amy MacDonald and Maureen Roffey (Candlewick Press, 1992)
Let's Play
Let's Make A Noise
Let's Do It
Let's Try

Babies by Moira Kemp and Matthew Price (Dell, 1991)

My Dad Is Awesome by Nick Butterworth (Candlestick Press, 1989)

*Match Patch Series: **Butterfly, Rabbit, Duck, Teddy*** (Yearling Books, 1991-92)

The *Spot Books* by Eric Hill (G. P. Putnam's Sons, 1980-1992):
Spot Looks At Opposites
Spot Counts From 1 To 10
Spot On The Farm
Spot At Home
Spot In The Garden
Spot's Toy Box

PERSONAL RECORD
Additional Titles, New Insights, Interesting Observations

_____

_____

_____

_____

_____

_____

_____

_____

_____

_____

_____

_____

_____

_____

_____

_____

_____

_____

_____

_____

_____

_____

_____

_____

_____

_____

6 READING (TO, WITH AND) BY CHILDREN

To this point, we have discussed how oral language develops, the stages of reading development and the ways in which parents and teachers can facilitate reading to and with children. As we make reading experiences priorities in our home and school environments, children move closer and closer to achieving independence in reading. They are able to read more and more material on their own. They move into the reading by stage. The quality of this stage is largely dependent on the persistence of effort demonstrated in the first two stages. Remember the rule of language: All performance is based on input.

The reading by stage generally becomes the focus when children are approximately five or six years old. The goal is to have children entering this stage just prior to or in the Kindergarten year. The emphasis in this stage is on having children read by themselves daily. Early in this stage, children read independently the books they have already mastered in the reading with stage . They continue to expand this number because they still are learning different selections during reading with sessions. The major point of the reading by stage is to provide much practice in print. This allows children to recognize a great number of words automatically and thus to develop fluency.

During the first few months that children are in this stage, it is suggested that you still read to them for about 30 minutes per day. Reading with and reading by children should share the second session. As children become more confident in reading, session one may be divided between reading to and with children and session two devoted to reading by children.

In the reading by stage, it may become necessary to reorganize your collection of books. I suggest that you have three baskets or crates. Place the books that you use for reading to, with and by in different containers. This greatly cuts down on the confusion of finding books that are appropriate for each level. (In our home, I bought three wicker laundry baskets in different colors. In one basket were all the books that were used for reading to my children. In another basket were all the books that were being used for reading with my children. In the last basket were the books that my children could read by themselves.)

In this stage, as children read by themselves, provide as much encouragement as they need. If they encounter words that they do not know, suggest that they spell the words and make the best attempt that they can. You may also encourage them to try sounding the first letter. As phonic skill increases, help them to sound more of the letters. Remember to model this skill as well. If they are not successful, provide the word. This is not the time to become impatient or to create a hostile or unpleasant environment.

As you involve children in reading by activities, vary the reading session by encouraging them to read one section or page and you read the other. In this way, you are providing good models as children listen to you read then practice their own skills.

During the reading by stage, it is important to continue to build the word banks, work with labeling the environment and especially to focus on alphabet and phonic work. It is suggested that during the reading by time, you spend approximately fifteen minutes on the reading of print and approximately the same amount of time doing word, alphabet or phonic work.

If at this point children are still experiencing difficulty remembering the letter forms (ie. this letter is "p" : this letter is "j") you need to provide more direct practice in this skill. Introduce more alphabet forms into the environment. For example, you can buy sponge, rubber or plastic letters for play in the bathtub. Get magnetic plastic letters and place them in a plastic bag for practice in the car. Buy placemats that have the alphabet and corresponding pictures on them and practice before, during or after meals. Read and discuss a stage three alphabet book every day. Remind children to visualize the pages. These suggestions are very cost effective. You can buy any of these items for very little money at any bargain store.

The key to success is the same as with any skill or activity. You must be convinced that reading is important and must be willing to spend the time to help your children learn. Your actions must show your children that reading is a significant value in your home.

As reading develops, you might want to begin an additional daily silent reading time during which children choose any material they wish and read quietly by themselves. This ought to be an established period by the time children reach the first grade. It need not be a long time. Ten to fifteen minutes will do.

Please also remember that although reading by is now the priority, reading to and with are both daily occurrences.

Once children are able to read a number of selections by themselves, reward and encourage them:
- Keep a chart of all the books they read. When they have read a predetermined number, reward them by doing something special.
- When they read a selection well, have them read it for someone who is special to them.
- Have them put favorite selections on tape and share them with family and friends.
- Have them put selections on tape and give tape/book gifts to younger relatives, friends or peers.
- Have them tape favorite stories as Christmas gifts for grandparents.

It is very important that children feel appreciated for their efforts. They are on a wonderful journey and should know that there are great rewards along the way.

Let us now review the activities that are part of each one of the three stages.

Reading To:

- We read to children daily.
- We read for two 30 minutes periods daily.
- We use the first session for the reading of factual material and the second session for the reading of narrative material.
- We read for a variety of purposes and read a wide range of material.
- We read favorite selections over and over. (It is a good habit to read books twice at one sitting.)
- We make reading a priority and try not to miss a day.
- We remember that reading to children does not have to be a totally quiet activity. We can read to them when they are getting ready for bed, when they are taking a bath, when they are eating, when they are resting or when they are waiting for an activity.
- We do not expect responses from children. We are content to fill up children's mental knowledge banks.

Reading With

- We still read to children for one session each day. We alternate factual and narrative reading during this session. During the second session, we read with children.
- During the reading with session, we reread many easy reading and predictable print books.
- We allow children to read familiar words and phrases with us.
- We use the to, with and by strategy liberally.
- We begin to keep word banks and word cards with children.
- We begin alphabet work.
- We start playing phonic games.
- We work with sound/concept tins.
- We label our environment and help children learn words.

- We interact with children and continuously help them to develop keen comprehension skills through our varied questioning and modeling.

Reading By

- Early in this stage, reading session one is devoted to reading to children. Later in the stage, reading to and with children share session one and session two is reserved for reading by children.
- Children read books they know to parents and to themselves.
- During the reading by time children read books and also do alphabet and word work.
- We continue to work on word banks, word cards, concept/sound tins, phonic games and environmental labeling.
- We reinforce the alphabet and sounds in the environment.
- We reward children for reading and provide many opportunities for them to share their books.
- We continue to develop comprehension through questions, modeling and encouraging visualization.

Adults are the most critical individuals in the lives of children. The environments that we create for them will eventually shape their value systems. We can indeed help our children to become literate and thus to make more rewarding their human destinies.

PERSONAL RECORD

Additional Titles, New Insights, Interesting Observations

_____

_____

_____

_____

_____

_____

_____

_____

_____

_____

_____

_____

_____

_____

_____

_____

_____

_____

_____

_____

_____

_____

_____

_____

7 A Personal Testimony

Throughout this book, I have been presenting and strongly recommending the To, With, By approach to the development of literacy. I feel very justified in my strong attachment to this approach because I have followed almost to the letter this sequence of activities twice; once with my son and again,very recently, with my step-daughter. On both occasions, we achieved tremendous success. In this chapter, I will share with you my personal experiences, in the hope that the process of literacy development will be seen for what it really is: a very meaningful and manageable goal.

I have been a professor of reading instruction for more than fifteen years. As such, I have had continuous exposure to the development of reading in both adults and children. Prior to 1986 however, I had never seen reading actually blossom from the total absence of it, to a high degree of competence in one person. In 1986, I had the opportunity to become intimately involved in watching reading unfold for my then three year old son.

I adopted my son in March of 1986. He was then three years and five months old. He had previously been in a wonderful, warm and loving foster home. He had a relatively good oral language base. However, he had not been in a strong print environment. He had not been read to a lot. He could not identify a favorite book or story. Although he could sing the alphabet song somewhat accurately, he could not identify any letters. He was also unable to read any words including his own name.

I had at that time very clear views related to literacy. First, I knew that learning to read begins long before one's first experiences with print. Personal and meaningful experiences with rich oral language are central to the development of reading. Second, I knew that because reading is so closely related to early oral language experiences, the most essential base of reading performance has its roots in the early home environment. Because of this, parents have a unique and irreplaceable role in the creation of a strong base for reading .

My views, in addition to my new opportunity for parenting, led me to make some important decisions.

- I would create and implement a home reading environment that would be conducive to literacy development.
- I would observe daily the unfolding of reading in my son, record in detail my findings and analyze these findings in order to come to some conclusions about early reading development.

What resulted from my experiment was extremely validating, informative and exciting. I created and applied a home based literacy program in which both my son and I were intimately involved. We began this journey into literacy in March of 1986. At that time, my son was a total nonreader. By the end of August, 1987, approximately seventeen months later, his reading level was mid third grade. More importantly, he loved to read, often reading forty or more pages of print per day.

Following is an accurate account of the events that led to this remarkable unfolding of literacy.

Reading To My Son: Building A Base For Literacy

Phase one of our journey into literacy began in March of 1986, and lasted for approximately ten months until mid February, 1987. For these ten months, I heavily concentrated on building as solid a base as possible for my son's oral language and reading development. Reading to him was my priority during this time.

I had five major goals as we embarked on this journey together. They were:

1. To support him in his love of language and his openness to learning. My son was and continues to be an eager learner. Although he had not yet begun to seek out print, he questioned his environment continuously, was extremely interested in sharing oral language and was willing to learn new information. I wanted to introduce print to him in such a way that his natural curiosity would remain intact, and his need to know would be continuously fed.

2. To provide my son with a broad base of information which would form a strong foundation for content comprehension.

   In order for my son to meet his future school demands, he would need to know much content. He would ultimately be exposed to information about families, libraries, schools, farms, countries, states, numbers, colors, animals, insects: all the experiences that make up his world. Reading to him would provide him with the content that would ensure his future comprehension.

3. To expose my son to a wide range of literature.

   I wanted my son to learn to read and to do so well. More importantly, however, I wanted him to be familiar with print in all forms and to feel comfortable with all types of written material. I wanted him to know about poetry, folk tales, drama, myths, history, biblical stories, nonfiction, legends and more. In my reading to him, I would include a wide range of print.

4. To observe my son's reactions to print and to identify his tastes and interests.

   We all, as human beings, tend to do best that which we like most. My son was no exception to this rule. I wanted to observe closely which content, literature, experiences and material he liked most. I would then be able to use his interests to lead him directly into reading.

5. To structure our home environment in such a way that the love of language would be the end result.

   I wanted my son to learn to read very well. Most important to me, however, was that he learn to love reading. I wanted him to possess not only the skills of reading, but also the motivation to read. I believed that this goal would best be accomplished by daily exposure to interesting, meaningful and appealing material.

   So intent was I on focusing on my goals that I had a list of them posted on my bathroom mirror as a daily reminder.

Accomplishing My Goals: Reading To My Son

Once my goals were established, I went about the task of creating a home environment that would have the greatest chance of fulfilling each goal. The most critical thing I had to do was to commit myself to daily reading times. I set aside two twenty to thirty minute reading sessions, one in the morning and one at night. I realized that on some days, it would not be possible to get them both in. However, I had that as a goal, and made every effort to reach my goal.

On many mornings, I would read to him as he ate breakfast. Often, I read to him for twenty minutes just after he woke up. On some mornings, we would have just enough time for five or ten minutes of reading. Often, we had to read for fifteen minutes before dinner because we couldn't fit it in that morning. We would then read again for twenty to thirty minutes just before bedtime. Because this was a priority for me, I worked with my available time and made a place for reading. I realized that it was better to read for five minutes in one session than to skip the session completely.

Our first reading session was devoted to factual material. I read books to my son following all the reading to rules that have been discussed in this workbook. We read books about colors, shapes, numbers, letters, reptiles, animals and the like. Among his favorite titles were the following:

The Animal World by E. K. Davis (A Golden Book, 1982)

Animal Homes by E. K. Davis (A Golden Book,1982)

Animals: Animal Information Books (Price, Stern and Sloan, 1984)
Titles include:
Birds
Bears
Farm Animals
Wild Animals

My First Book About Space by Dinah L. Moche (A Golden Book, 1982)

Dinosaurs: A Lost World by Keith Mosley (G. P. Putnam's Sons, 1984)

Our Amazing World: Fascinating Facts (Brimax Books Ltd., 1986)

All About Dinosaurs (Derrydale Books, 1985)

The A B C Bunny by Wanda Gag (Coward McCann Inc., 1933)

Little Simon A B C by Mike Brown (Simon and Schuster, 1982)

My First Book Of Shapes
My First Book Of Words
My First Book Of Colors
My First Book Of Numbers
All By Eric Carle (Thomas Crowell, 1974)

These books were read to him many, many times during the seventeen months.

Our second session was devoted to the reading of narrative material. It usually took place just before bedtime. During this time, I read fiction of all types. His favorite titles follow:

Whistle For Willie by Ezra Jack Keats (Puffin Books, 1985)

Peter's Chair by Ezra Jack Keats (Harper and Row, 1967)

The Snowy Day by Ezra Jack Keats (Puffin Books, 1986)

Teddy In The Garden by Amanda Davidson (Holt, Rinehart and Winston, 1986)

Where The Wild Things Are by Maurice Sendak (Harper and Row, 1963)

The Friendly Beasts by Tomie de Paola (G. P. Putnam's Sons, 1981)

Never Hit A Porcupine by Barbara Williams (E. P. Dutton, 1977)

Goodnight Moon by Margaret Wise Brown (Harper and Row, 1975)

Brown Bear, Brown Bear, What Do You See? by Bill Martin Junior (Holt, Rinehart and Winston, 1967)

The Baby's Story Book by Kay Chorao (E. P. Dutton, 1985)

Young Joe by Jan Ormerod (Lothrop, Lee and Shepard, 1986)

The Very Hungry Caterpillar by Eric Carle (Philomel Books, 1981)

Oh, The Thinks You Can Think by Dr. Seuss (Beginner Books, Random House, 1975)

The Ghost Eye Tree by Bill Martin Junior (Holt, Rinehart and Winston, 1986)

The Haunted House by Dorothy Rose (Simon and Schuster Inc., 1986)

Pumpkin, Pumpkin by Jeanne Titherington (Greenwillow Books, 1986)

Papa, Please Get The Moon For Me by Eric Carle (Picture Book Studio U.S.A., 1986)

Leo The Late Bloomer by Robert Kraus (Windmill Books, 1971)

Follow That Bird by Sesame Street (Random House , 1985)

When I'm Sleepy by Jane Howard (E. P. Dutton, 1985)

The Napping House by Audrey Wood (Harcourt, Brace & Jovanovich, 1984)

How Joe The Bear And Sam The Mouse Got Together by Beatrice Schenk De Regniers (Scholastic Book Services, 1965)

Mother Goose by Michael Hague (Holt, Rinehart and Winston, 1984)

Abiyoyo by Pete Seeger (Macmillan, 1986)

During session one, I usually read one selection and during session two, I read at least two selections. Throughout these sessions, I made certain resolutions:

1. I would not require my son to respond to what I was reading. I answered all his questions, pointed out interesting facts and reacted to all his comments. I did not ask any specific questions to check the level of his comprehension unless that was my specific purpose for reading. My focus was on exposing him to repeated experiences with a wide variety of print.

2. I would not force my son to look at the print. For the vast majority of the time, however, he chose to do so. Often, especially during session two, he was in bed or was painting or coloring. I wanted him to become immersed in hearing the language of print.

3. Regardless of how many times my son chose to hear the same selection, I would (as pleasantly as possible) reread it. This was often difficult, because there were books that he chose to hear at least once per day for several months. It was important for me to remember that during the reading to stage, children need a significant number of repetitions in order to build a strong language base. Late in stage one, when I felt that I couldn't read a book one more time, I made a tape recording of the book and had my son listen to it at bedtime. This worked out very well.

4. I would read to my son every day. Reading would be a priority in our home. At least one session would be kept every single day. I realized that just as oral language is essential every day, so is written language.

Preparing For Reading

My experiences in this stage taught me a great deal about my son. First, he loved print. He loved being read to. He loved hearing about characters, places and things. He gravitated toward books with clear conversation, definite language patterns and strong emotional content. He also loved books about animals.

For the first four or five months, he was not interested in sitting still and listening, except in the second session when he was ready for bed. Typically, he would ask a few questions for clarification. Mainly, I read a lot and he listened. After approximately five months, however, he became much more attentive and interested. He began to ask more questions, to make comments related to the content and to look at the illustrations as I read.

By mid October, 1986, seven months into stage one, I noticed that he was becoming much more interested in print itself and was asking many questions about the selections. He had also started to memorize sections of many books and would spontaneously read with me when passages were familiar. It was at this time that I began deleting words and passages that he knew, running my fingers under the deleted sections and encouraging him to "read" them.

By mid November, 1986, my son had memorized fifteen books. When I read these books, he spontaneously recited them with me and turned the pages by himself at the appropriate times. He was still looking primarily at the pictures, however, and not at the print. The fifteen books he had memorized were:

Brown Bear, Brown Bear, What Do You See? by Bill Martin Junior (Holt, 1967)

Goodnight Moon by Margaret Wise Brown (Harper and Row, 1975)

Young Joe by Jan Ormerod (Lothrop, Lee and Shepard, 1986)

The Very Hungry Caterpillar by Eric Carle (Philomel Books, 1981)

I Know An Old Lady by Rose Bonne (Scholastic Book Services, 1968)

Pumpkin, Pumpkin by Jeanne Titherington (Greenwillow Books, 1986)

When I'm Sleepy by Jane Howard (E. P. Dutton, 1985)

The Napping House by Audrey Wood (Harcourt, Brace and Jovanovich, 1984)

The A B C Bunny by Wanda Gag (Coward, McCann, 1933)

My First Book Of Words by Eric Carle (Thomas Crowell, 1974)

My First Book Of Shapes by Eric Carle (Thomas Crowell, 1974)

My First Book Of Numbers by Eric Carle (Thomas Crowell, 1974)

My A B C Book by Tadasu Yzawa (Grosset and Dunlap, 1971)

My Book Of Prayers by Francis Carfi Matranga (five prayers) (The Standard Publishing Co., 1985)

Ed Emberly's A B C by Ed Emberly (Little, Brown and Co., 1978)

All these books contained repeated language patterns. Routinely, as I read them, my son would join in and "say" the books with me. During this period, he repeated them around the house, in the car, in the bathtub, at the store and even at church. He would often say to me as we were traveling in the car, "Mommy, do you want me to read a book for you?" He would then proceed to "read" one of his memorized books beautifully, without the presence of the book. The solid foundation for reading was being built.

By December, 1986, I noticed that my son was becoming increasingly inquisitive about actual print. He began asking questions such as, " Which word says ——? What is this word? Does this word say——? What word spells——?" These questions were always asked about books with which he was very familiar or that he had memorized. As these questions began to be asked very frequently, I knew that he was ready for another small step toward reading. I began preparing for phase two, reading with my son.

By January,1987, I began the transition into reading with my son. I emphasized predictable print books, easy reading books and alphabet books. Once a day, every day, I read at least one predictable print book, one easy reading book, (a short book with very few words in large print on each page) and one stage three alphabet book to my son. I focused on a single stage three alphabet book and began to work toward alphabet recognition.

Because the alphabet was becoming important, I began to introduce letters and words into our home. I bought placemats with the alphabet, colors and numbers. We talked about the letters as we waited for meals. I placed an alphabet poster in my son's room. We sang the alphabet song and looked at each letter as we got dressed in the morning and at night. I bought a set of sponge letters for the bathtub, and we played with them at bathtime. I bought a set of plastic letters for our toy box which was kept in the car. During this time, I made no attempt to have my son produce, although he almost always joined me as I read or talked about the alphabet. I was still giving information to him and filling up his knowledge bank.

I was, at that time, reading to my son twice a day. During the first session, I read nonfiction material, and during the second session, I read narrative material. However, because session two now included so many predictable print, easy reading and alphabet books, several of his favorite books and many new selections were not being read. I therefore put new books and his old favorites that had been somewhat ignored, on tape for him. At naptime and at night, he fell asleep to one of these selections.

To this point, I noticed that my son recognized many words "in context". By February, 1987, he was "reading" memorized books independently. He often pointed to words accurately as he read. I was not sure how many words he knew in isolation, but I knew that the process of word recognition had definitely begun.

Phase two, reading with my son, clearly began on February 15, 1987. On that day, I was baking pumpkin cupcakes for dinner, when my son looked at the recipe and said, "Mommy, look! Pumpkin, pumpkin, just like in my *Pumpkin, Pumpkin* book." He had recognized his first word outside of the context of his own books. That very evening, we moved into stage two, reading with my son.

Reading (To And) With My Son

Beginning in mid February, 1987, we started the reading with stage. First, I changed the structure of the reading sessions. I read factual and narrative material to my son during the first session. During the second session, I read predictable print, easy reading and alphabet books with him. I followed the reading with rules discussed earlier in this book.

I began environmental labeling in my son's room. I started with ten words and eventually built up to forty words. I created a word bank for my son. We placed all the known words from his memorized books in this word bank and added to it as new words were learned. We practiced these words daily. My son often chose to bring his word bank with him in the car, to church or to any meetings we attended.

As I read books, I omitted those words that he knew and had him read them by himself. I read very easy reading books to and with him, then had him read the books back to me. I placed all the books that he could read fluently and independently in a reading basket and left them in his bedroom. At night, after our reading with time, I gave my son an extra five or ten minutes to read to himself. He relished this time because it made him feel grown up to stay up later than his assigned bedtime.

One very useful set of materials we used during this stage was the Questron Electronic Quiz Book Series, Price, Stern and Sloan, distributed by Random House Inc., 1983 to 1985. These are books that range from preschool to adult levels. They are electronically coded to be used with the Questron wand. This wand allows one to select answers to questions and provides immediate sound responses to correct and incorrect answers. My son absolutely loved these materials. His favorite titles were:

My First Counting Book
My First A B C Book
My First Book Of Animals

Shapes And Sizes
My First Numbers
My First Words
My First Nursery Rhymes
Reading Readiness

My son would play with this series for hours at a time.

We began alphabet work during this period. We started visualizing the stage three alphabet book, *On Market Street* by Arnold Lobel, Mulberry Books, 1981. We did alphabet work every day.

By June of 1987, my son could read approximately thirty two books independently. He was actually recognizing the words, not just repeating the texts from memory. These thirty two books included the fifteen selections that my son had memorized in the reading to stage months earlier.

By the end of June, 1987, I started to reproduce on plain white paper, the words of the books my son could read independently. Each day, we read one or two known books with and without pictures. During this time, I could really see a tremendous growth in the number of words my son could recognize independently. He had over 180 words in his word bank. At this point, we removed all those words that he knew automatically and kept only those that needed further practice.

By late June, 1987, we advanced our alphabet work by beginning to separate individual sounds (A is for Apple, /a/ /a/ /a/ Apple). We practiced this skill for about three to five minutes daily.

In August, 1987, my son was four years and ten months old. He loved to read! During the second week of August, he began to sound out unfamiliar words independently. I had just purchased the book, *The Big Little Golden Book Of Planets* (Golden Books, 1987). I had planned to introduce it to him sometime during that week. As I was busy doing some school work, he came running into my office with the book in his hands. " Is this *The Big Little Golden Book Of Planets* mine, Mom?" he asked. Almost without thinking, I told him that it was. Then, it hit me. He had read the title all by himself! We certainly celebrated that evening. I could see the results of our journey into literacy right before my eyes. My son had become a real reader. I cannot say that I did not see this coming. It began seventeen months before when we began our journey into literacy. There were glimpses of it when he began to memorize his first books. There were clear signs when he learned his first words by memory. However, it seemed that overnight, my son became a reader. He not only learned and understood print, but he was able to figure out unknown words on his own. It was time to move into the third stage of reading by my son.

Reading (To, With and) By My Son

My son started kindergarten at a private school in early September of 1987. He was four years and eleven months old at that time. Placement testing indicated that his overall reading level was close to mid third grade. We moved into the reading by stage at this time. Each day, I read to my son for approximately thirty minutes. I also read with him and had him read by himself for about thirty minutes. During the reading with session, we read easy reading books daily. I began to create sound/ concept tins and concentrated on phonic work. I still practiced to, with and by reading.

I instituted an independent reading period for ten to fifteen minutes each day. During this time, my son read books of his own choice. After each session, we discussed what he had read.

By the end of his kindergarten year, his reading was improving by leaps and bounds. His phonic knowledge was growing. His comprehension was excellent. He was really a quite literate person. He could name his favorite authors, illustrators and types of writing. Our journey into literacy had been a great success!

My son is now nine years old. He is an avid reader. His reading level is approximately five years above his grade placement. Each summer, he reads a minimum of one hundred books. Of course, this is made easier because our family requires each of our children to read for one hour every day. My son is proof that the system explained in this workbook does work. However, it requires a great deal of commitment on the part of adults.

8 IN THE FINAL ANALYSIS

If you have sacrificed both the money and the time to buy and to read this book, you certainly do not need to be convinced of the importance of literacy in general and of reading in particular in our society. Our children of today will be the workers of tomorrow. We are in the tide of the technological age in which literacy demands are at an all time high. In order to claim their futures, our children will need to master the skills of reading and thinking. It is unwise to believe that schools can single-handedly meet all the literacy needs of children.

Children's values are primarily formed by three major groups of individuals: parents, teachers and peers. The first group that they encounter is parents. Parents set the initial value system to which children are exposed. Parents create the environments that foster and nurture children's first views of the world. In terms of literacy, parents set the stage for literacy or for the absence of literacy. It is parents that first create the love of reading, the value of print, the love of learning, the expansion of information and the development of language in children.

The first five or six years that children spend at home are critical in their literacy development. Regardless of how excellent schools are, they are not able to provide this initial literacy experience to the extent that children need it. It is the home environment that has the responsibility for the building of strong foundations in oral language, vocabulary, information, thinking skills, concepts and literacy.

When children come to school with the foundations of language and literacy, then teachers have the opportunity to use the foundations in the building of academic skills and content. Without those strong foundations, however, teachers must take the time to do the jobs of parents prior to the direct presentation of the curriculum.

If we as parents take a realistic look at the educational system, especially at the early elementary levels, it would be easy to see that the job of teachers is an almost impossible one. Let me illustrate this point by taking a look at the reading instructional block in most schools.

Let us assume that in a first grade classroom, reading is focused on for two and one half hours daily. Let us further assume that there are four different kinds of readers in that classroom: pre readers who know no words or phonic skills at all; beginning readers who know a few words, the alphabet forms, but no sounds; early readers who can read easy reading texts quite well; and mature readers who read at least two years above their grade placement. Let us say that the teacher spends daily time instructing each group. This means that each group would have approximately forty minutes of instruction daily. Let us allow five minutes of passing time between groups. Now we are down to about thirty five minutes of instruction for each group. Let us further assume that given the children's young age, teachers would need five minutes per group to deal with behavioral issues. Now we are down to thirty minutes of instruction. Now let us assume that there are six children in each group and that the teacher spends approximately the same time focusing on each child. That means that each child gets about five minutes of direct individualized attention each day. This is, of course, if there are no unexpected interruptions whatever.

As a parent, then, I must ask myself the question, "Can my child's literacy needs be completely met by one teacher in one school?" Personally, my answer is, "Absolutely not!" regardless of how outstanding the teacher may be. As a parent, I must also ask myself the question, " In which group do I want my child?" I must realize that the answer is to a large degree up to me. My child's performance does have a lot to do with the kinds of experiences I have provided for her or him since birth. It is not reasonable to think that one teacher can produce the same results with twenty five very different learners, that one or two parents can produce with one, two, four, five or even six children.

In the final analysis, the fact is that all of us as adults need to work together to meet the needs of all our children.

Parents must construct foundations that support and nurture literacy and teachers must build on those foundations and extend them to support the needs of the ever expanding curriculum. If we all work together, the beneficiaries will be the keepers of tomorrow, our children. **I wish you all the conviction to believe in, the courage to embark on and the commitment to complete this important and rewarding journey into literacy.**

THE END

Barbara Swaby is a professor of Education at the University of Colorado at
Colorado Springs. She is the director of the graduate reading program and the
graduate reading clinic. She has taught courses in reading instruction for
approximately thirty years. She is the author of several articles, two textbooks,
two workbooks, a set of readers for beginning readers and four children's books.
She is married and has one son and two step-daughters.